DESTINATION
Middle Ages

Your Guide to Trade in the Middle Ages

James Bow

Crabtree Publishing Company
www.crabtreebooks.com

Crabtree Publishing Company

www.crabtreebooks.com

Author: James Bow

Managing Editor: Tim Cooke

Designer: Lynne Lennon

Picture Manager: Sophie Mortimer

Design Manager: Keith Davis

Editorial Director: Lindsey Lowe

Children's Publisher: Anne O'Daly

Editor: Petrice Custance

Proofreader: Wendy Scavuzzo

**Production coordinator
  and prepress technician:** Tammy McGarr

Print coordinator: Margaret Amy Salter

Written and produced for Crabtree Publishing Company
by Brown Bear Books

Photographs (t=top, b=bottom, l=left, r=right, c=center):
Front Cover: 123rf: Fedor Selivanov br; **Alamy:** Peter Horree cr;
Public Domain: Gemaldegalerie, Berlin tr, Office de Tourisme du
Grand Troyes cr.

Interior: 123rf: Dmitry Knorre 12r, Yang Yu 22l; **Alamy:** 9b, CWIS
28, Bernard O'Kane 9tr; **Bridgeman Art Library:** 12bl, 13b, 19, 27l,
Bibliotheque Nationale de Paris 15t, British Library Board 25r;
British Library: 18bl; **Dreamstime:** 18r, Patryk Kosmider 17t; **Getty
Images:** Leemage 26bl; **Public Domain:** 29t, Bibliotheque Nationale
de Paris 8, KBWEi 10bl, Kunsthalle, Hamburg 20r, Alte Pinakothek
23b; **Rijksmuseum:** Koninklijk Oudheidkundig Genootschap 14;
Shutterstock: 5b, 20c, Tony Baggett 13t, Canadastock 10tr, Claudio
Giovanni Columbo 22br, Eric Isselée 21t, Rosa Jay 11t, Oscar Johns
23c, lightpoet 16br, Boris Stroujko 26r, Po Wen 29b; **Thinkstock:**
istockphoto 11b, 17b, 20br, 25l, Photos.com 15b, 27br; **Topfoto:** The
Granger Collection 4, 16l, 21l, World History Archive 5t.

All other photos, artwork and maps, **Brown Bear Books**.

Brown Bear Books has made every attempt to contact the
copyright holder. If you have any information please contact
licensing@brownbearbooks.co.uk

Library and Archives Canada Cataloguing in Publication

Bow, James, 1972-, author
    Your guide to trade in the Middle Ages / James Bow.

(Destination: Middle Ages)
Includes index.
Issued in print and electronic formats.
ISBN 978-0-7787-2996-9 (hardcover).--
ISBN 978-0-7787-3052-1 (softcover).--
ISBN 978-1-4271-1869-1 (HTML)

    1. Commerce--History--Medieval, 500-1500--Juvenile literature.
2. Trade routes--History--To 1500--Juvenile literature. I. Title.

HF395.B69 2017   j380.9'02   C2016-907401-3
                                           C2016-907402-1

Library of Congress Cataloging-in-Publication Data

CIP is available at the Library of Congress

Crabtree Publishing Company

www.crabtreebooks.com   1-800-387-7650

Printed in Canada/032017/BF20170111

Published in Canada
Crabtree Publishing
616 Welland Ave.
St. Catharines, ON
L2M 5V6

Published in the United States
Crabtree Publishing
PMB 59051
350 Fifth Avenue, 59th Floor
New York, New York 10118

Published in the United Kingdom
Crabtree Publishing
Maritime House
Basin Road North, Hove
BN41 1WR

Published in Australia
Crabtree Publishing
3 Charles Street
Coburg North
VIC, 3058

Contents

Before We Start

The early Middle Ages in Europe was a period of very little trade, learning, or artistic achievement, and is sometimes referred to as the "Dark Ages." By around 1000 C.E., however, conditions began to improve.

AFTER THE FALL OF ROME

+ **Europe at war**

The Middle Ages describes the 1,000-year period following the end of the Roman Empire in 476. Before that time, Rome controlled most of Europe and the Mediterranean Sea. Its empire had wealthy cities, and people traded widely. After the end of the Roman Empire, Europe split into warring kingdoms. They fought each other more often than they traded with each other.

ON THE LAND

✦ **Farming and associated trades...**

✦ **...keep everyone busy**

Most medieval Europeans worked on the land. They farmed or did jobs connected with making tools, baking bread, butchering animals, or making things from wood (above). Most people were peasants. They worked for a lord or knight, who let the peasants farm a portion of their land in return for the peasants' labor. Male peasants also had to serve in their lord's army, if called upon to do so.

GROWTH OF TOWNS

☛ Can feudal society survive?

Medieval Europe was a **feudal society**. The king owned the land, and shared it out among his **nobles**. The nobles in turn shared their land among lesser lords and knights. Peasants worked for these lords and knights in return for housing and protection. Peasants who had spare crops to sell took them to market in towns. Towns grew larger and more people moved there. These townspeople were outside the old feudal society. They did not depend on a lord for their living.

EUROPE AND THE WORLD

✦ Changes in the East

While European trade declined in the Dark Ages, new powers were rising in other parts of the world. In the 600s, a new religion called Islam began in Arabia. An Islamic Empire soon spread across the Middle East, North Africa, and Portugal and Spain. Farther east, China's empire was conquered by the Mongol leader Genghis Khan (left). Eventually, the Mongol Empire spread Chinese influence across Asia and into Europe.

COMING OF THE MERCHANTS

✦ Selling goods, making money

In the later Middle Ages, a new class of people started to appear in Europe's towns and cities. They were **merchants**, who bought and sold goods. They traveled to other towns or countries to find unusual goods to sell. Some became rich. Their money gave them political power. Towns also attracted craftspeople who made tools, clothes, or armor. They set up **guilds** to control their trades.

Where in the World?

Traders in some parts of Europe traded widely throughout the continent. Trade routes crossed Europe, and linked Europe to the Islamic Empire, India, and East Asia.

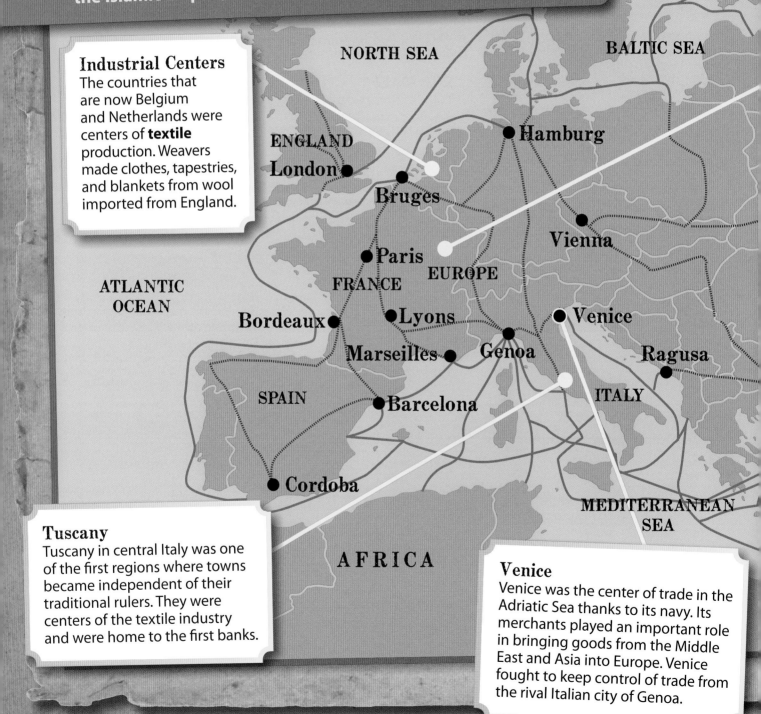

Industrial Centers

The countries that are now Belgium and Netherlands were centers of **textile** production. Weavers made clothes, tapestries, and blankets from wool imported from England.

NORTH SEA

BALTIC SEA

ENGLAND

London

Hamburg

Bruges

Vienna

Paris

EUROPE

FRANCE

ATLANTIC OCEAN

Bordeaux

Lyons

Venice

Marseilles

Genoa

Ragusa

SPAIN

Barcelona

ITALY

Cordoba

MEDITERRANEAN SEA

AFRICA

Tuscany

Tuscany in central Italy was one of the first regions where towns became independent of their traditional rulers. They were centers of the textile industry and were home to the first banks.

Venice

Venice was the center of trade in the Adriatic Sea thanks to its navy. Its merchants played an important role in bringing goods from the Middle East and Asia into Europe. Venice fought to keep control of trade from the rival Italian city of Genoa.

Champagne

The towns of the Champagne district of northeast France held six trade fairs each year. The fairs attracted many merchants. Champagne was on a crossroads of routes leading north–south and east–west across Europe, so it was relatively easy for merchants to travel there.

Silk Road

The Silk Road was really a whole system of routes for merchants from what is now Turkey to China. Few people traveled the whole route themselves. Goods passed from merchant to merchant along the route.

RUSSIA

Kiev

Key
—— Sea Routes
.... Land Routes

BLACK SEA

Constantinople

OTTOMAN EMPIRE

Antioch

To EAST ASIA

To INDIA

ISLAMIC EMPIRE

Constantinople

Constantinople was the capital of the Byzantine Empire. It stood at the western end of a long series of trade routes known as the Silk Road. These trade routes brought goods from East Asia to Europe, including Chinese silk. Constantinople was a powerful trading port until it was captured by the Muslim Ottoman Turks in 1453.

New Names
This map shows the modern names of countries. Most of these states did not exist in the Middle Ages.

Who We'll Meet

The travels and deals of some medieval traders and merchants made them famous during their lifetimes. Their influence on history is still felt today.

Making a Name

We know the names of several medieval merchants. This is because many of them could read and write. They wrote about their trade deals.

A CUNNING MERCHANT

✦ **Lyons makes enemies...**

✦ **...pays with his head**

Richard Lyons (d. 1381) was an English merchant who made a fortune from **fraudulent** deals. He became **sheriff** of London in 1375. King Edward III put him in charge of the **Mint**, but Lyons was fired for using his position to make dishonest loans. Many English people resented Lyons for his illegal deals. Lyons later became a member of Parliament. In 1381, English peasants revolted against high taxes. They marched to London to meet the king. They captured and beheaded Lyons. One reason for this may have been that he had once mistreated the peasants' leader, Wat Tyler.

BREAKING NEWS

If you are a king who can't raise enough money from your peasants to fight a war, take out a bank loan! Since 1164, the Bardi family in Florence has loaned money to Europe's kings. They expect the money back, with **interest**, after your victory. The Bardis went **bankrupt** in 1345, when England's King Edward III lost the Hundred Years' War to France. He could not pay his debts. Luckily, the Bardis have powerful friends to help get them back on their feet.

THE MERCHANT BECOMES EMIR

☞ The Strongman of Egypt

A Mongol by birth, Qawsun (1302–1342) arrived in Egypt as a trader. He set up in Cairo, selling leather goods. Qawsun was well educated, and became an advisor of the sultan, an-Nasir Muhammad. When an-Nasir died, Qawsun ruled on behalf of the sultan's young son. Qawsun was a strong ruler, who was known as the Strongman of Egypt. His enemies went to war against him. Qawsun was executed by the new sultan, and was buried in a grand tomb (right).

My Medieval Journal

Imagine you are the young Marco Polo. Your mother has died, and your father is about to set off on a long trip to China. Write to your father giving him reasons why he should take you along. How do you think you could be useful?

MARCO POLO'S GREAT ADVENTURE

+ From Venice to China

Marco Polo (c. 1254–1324) was the most famous of all medieval merchants. He was born to a family of traders in Venice while his father Niccolò was visiting China. When Marco's mother died, Marco was raised by relatives. Niccolò returned to Venice when Marco was 17. Marco joined his father's expedition (left). They traveled east, through the Middle East and the Himalayas, to the mysterious country of China. Marco stayed there for many years.

A Little Bit of History

In the early Middle Ages, most people worked on the land. There was little chance for anyone to change their place in society. However, from around the 1000s, this began to change.

GROWTH OF TOWNS

☛ **New trade centers...**

☛ **...get new powers**

During the early Middle Ages, there was little trade. Trade began to increase after about 1000. Towns such as Siena in Italy (right) became gathering places for traders. People in towns and cities began to reject the feudal system. Traders and merchants set up guilds to control trade, and formed town governments. Kings and lords benefited from taxing trade, so they were happy to encourage the growth of towns. They granted towns their own **charters**, giving citizens some rights to govern themselves.

THE TRADE FAIRS

+ **Everyone's gone to Champagne**

+ **The place to be seen**

In the 1100s, six market towns in the Champagne region of northern France held annual trade fairs. The region was conveniently located on rivers and old Roman roads. The fairs attracted traders from all over Europe. Cloth and leather merchants from the north met dye-makers and spice-traders from the south. To store all the goods, huge warehouses, or storage buildings, were built. The buildings can still be seen in the region today (left).

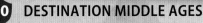

DEATH FROM THE EAST

+ Plague spread by rats

+ Millions die

The disease known as the Black Death began in Central Asia in 1343. It arrived in Europe in 1347. It was carried by fleas on rats (below). By 1353, up to 200 million people had died. Crops failed because there were not enough people to harvest them. When the **plague** was over, there was a shortage of people to work. **Tradespeople** could charge more for their labor. Peasants left their feudal lords to work for whoever would pay them the most.

NEWS FROM AFAR

The merchant Marco Polo returned to Italy from China in 1295. He was jailed in Genoa, which was trying to disrupt Venetian trade. In jail, Marco described China to another prisoner, Rustichello da Pisa. Rustichello wrote Marco's words down in *The Travels of Marco Polo*. The book became a bestseller.

To America

Marco Polo's stories of China encouraged explorers to head to East Asia. One explorer, Christopher Columbus, reached the Americas instead.

FULL SAIL AHEAD

+ New vessels for trading

+ Also useful for exploration

Caravels and carracks were two new types of ships developed during the later Middle Ages. The carrack was a large vessel with square sails. The caravel was lighter and faster. The caravel had triangular sails that could be moved easily to catch the wind. Caravels and carracks were very stable in rough oceans. Explorers used the vessels to cross the Atlantic Ocean. Traders used the ships to carry cargoes to Europe from the Americas, and from south and southeast Asia.

Get a Job!

In the Middle Ages, it became possible for the first time for people to choose how they made a living. There were many different choices on offer.

SELL YOUR SKILLS

+ New trades appear

One important job in the Middle Ages was being a blacksmith. Blacksmiths worked in a **forge** and used a hammer to make horseshoes, armor, and swords out of softened iron. Bowyers carved and bent wood to make bows and arrows. Millers in watermills or windmills (right) ground grain into flour. Coopers made barrels from strips of wood. Trades developed to make almost anything.

BUYING AND SELLING

✦ Merchants hit the road

While tradespeople rarely traveled, merchants visited new places. They bought things that were in short supply or unknown at home, such as spices, textiles, furs, glass, and jewelry. Merchants bought goods cheaply and sold them for a profit. They often made a good living. But they always risked losing their merchandise to thieves or shipwrecks.

POWER OF THE GUILDS

☛ Trade secrets...

☛ ... closely guarded

People who wanted to learn a trade had to join a guild. Guilds helped tradespeople prevent other people from learning their skills. It took years to learn a trade. Tradespeople hired children, who worked as **apprentices** while they learned the craft. After several years, an apprentice created a "masterpiece" in the hope that the guild would accept him as a master craftsman. Guilds grew wealthy. They built impressive headquarters (right).

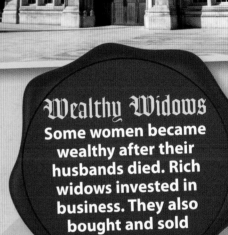

> *Those that are hired by the day leave off work at the first ringing of vespers [evening service] of Notre Dame.*
>
> **Rules of the Fullers' [Dyers'] Guild in Paris**

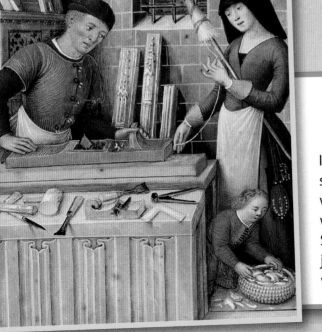

Wealthy Widows

Some women became wealthy after their husbands died. Rich widows invested in business. They also bought and sold property.

WOMEN AT WORK

+ Learning a trade

In feudal times, women were expected to do tasks at home such as cooking, weaving, and knitting. However, many women also worked outside the home. Daughters and wives learned the trades of their fathers and husbands. Some even joined guilds. Unmarried women had to take jobs in domestic service to support themselves. They worked as maids or cooks in people's homes.

Urban Jungles

In the 1000s, increased trade led to a rapid growth of towns. There were more towns than previously, and many were wealthy.

MOVING TO THE TOWNS

+ **Houses and workshops**

+ **And money to spend!**

Towns were initially places where peasants met to sell the crops they had grown and to buy supplies. Tradespeople set up stores to make tools, clothes, or craft goods. For many people, the family home was right above the store. The tools made by traders helped other people work more productively. In that way, business made everyone richer. There was more money to spend, which meant more business and wealth in the towns (right).

THE NEW PROFESSIONS

✦ **Selling knowledge, not goods**

Towns and cities were centers for people who belonged to the professions, which meant jobs that required high levels of education and training. Professionals sold their knowledge rather than goods. There were only three professions in the Middle Ages. Divinity included all members of the clergy, medicine included doctors and surgeons, and the law included barristers and solicitors. People headed to towns for medical and legal advice.

My Medieval Journal

Imagine you are a medieval peasant used to living in the countryside. You have moved to a town to look for work. Using information from this book, write a letter home giving your impressions of the differences between life in the country and life in town.

Towns sprang up where roads or rivers (below) made it easy to trade. Growing towns caused problems, however. Many people crowded into narrow, cramped streets. The streets became dirty, the water became polluted, and sickness spread. Traders arriving from far away sometimes carried diseases. This often caused **epidemics** among the townspeople.

A CITY BUILT ON TRADE

+ **Venice rules the Adriatic**

The Italian city of Venice (below right) grew rich on trade. From the 800s to the 1100s, Venice's position on the Adriatic Sea gave it control over all the towns around the coast. Venetian ships traded with the Byzantine and Islamic empires. Merchants shipped valuable goods to Europe. The Adriatic was full of pirates. Venice's navy protected merchants' ships so they could reach Europe safely. Venice's rival was another Italian trading city—Genoa. The two cities fought five wars over trade between 1256 and 1381.

A Merchant's Life

A merchant spent much of his life on the road. Merchants visited distant markets, where they traded with other merchants who had also traveled great distances. This allowed merchants to buy goods from all over the world.

At the Inn

In towns, inns offered merchants beds, food, and entertainment. Hostlers provided stables to house the travelers' horses.

GO BY WATER

+ Rivers are natural highways

+ They lead to higher profits!

In the Middle Ages, rivers were natural highways. Most land routes were muddy footpaths or old Roman roads that provided a slow, bumpy ride. River travel was quicker, so merchants could get their goods to market faster. Towns on the coast or on rivers had harbors and docks (left). Ships unloaded goods there. The goods were taken to other towns on smaller ships or by road.

AVOIDING DANGER

✦ It's worth paying...
✦ ...to travel safely

It was risky being a merchant—and sometimes expensive! They had to pay for safe lodgings. They also had to pay fees called tolls to the people who owned bridges or roads. Bridges had booths or towers where tolls were collected (right). At sea, merchants risked storms and pirates. On land, they risked being robbed by thieves.

☛ **A welcome for traders**

☛ **Specialized facilities**

Sea ports offered safe harbors for ships to unload their cargoes (left). Trades developed around shipbuilding, dock work, and warehousing. Ships' captains and crews could be hired at the ports. There were always people looking for work. Ports such as London, Venice, and Marseilles attracted sailors from around the world. These ports became the meeting places for different nationalities.

Did you know?

European explorers tried to find new sea routes to Asia. The overland trade was controlled by Muslim traders in Central Asia. Europeans wanted to avoid them.

LONG-DISTANCE TRADE

+ **Building larger ships**

+ **Conquering other countries**

For merchants, the farther they could bring goods to sell, the more money they could charge for them. Merchants built larger ships such as caravels and carracks. These ships could not only hold more goods, they could also travel farther. Merchants seeking an easier route to the spices (right) of India and the silks of China sailed south and west in the Atlantic. They mapped the coast of Africa and eventually reached America. For the citizens of the places merchants visited, however, the results were often damaging. European traders were followed by soldiers as European countries began to settle **colonies** around the world.

Fair Trade

During the Middle Ages, a number of new developments made it easier for merchants and traders to do business with each other.

MAKING MORE MONEY

☛ Swapsies bites the dust

Bartering, or swapping goods for other goods, does not work if one person does not want what the other person has to trade. Money can be traded for whatever anyone wants. As merchants began to trade more goods, they began to deal in more money. The money was gold and silver coins (right) or paper representing promised amounts of gold and silver.

THE FIRST BANKS

+ Banks emerge in Italy

+ Make international trade easier

Money was more convenient than bartering. However, gold and silver were heavy to transport and easy to lose. The first banks (left) were created to keep money safe. Bankers stored gold safely in exchange for taking a small amount of it as payment. They gave merchants promissory notes, which were official notes stating how much gold the merchant had in the bank. Such notes were the basis of the paper money we use today. Paper money already existed in China. Marco Polo had seen it on his travels.

BREAKING NEWS

Everyone knows that Europeans rely on Muslim traders for goods from Asia, such as spices, gold, and porcelain. That's how ports such as Venice, Naples, and Genoa have grown rich. But there are signs things are changing. Now that Europe is emerging from the Dark Ages, more Europeans want to cut out Muslim middlemen and trade directly with the world.

My Medieval Journal

The medieval church said it was a sin to charge interest on a loan of money. Using evidence from this book, make an argument about how loans were necessary for helping medieval merchants conduct their business projects.

A KEY ROLE

☛ Jews lend money

Guilds barred Jews from most trades. As Jews were not Christians, however, Catholic rules against lending money for interest did not apply to them. Some Jews became money lenders. They loaned cash to traders. This launched the **stereotype** of Jewish people being greedy, which was used as a justification to **persecute** Jews.

CAN YOU SPARE A DIME?
✦ **Money lenders...**
✦ **... break Church rules**

Bankers loaned some of the money in their banks to people who needed it. The borrower promised to pay the money back with interest before the money's original owners needed it. This meant people could raise funds to invest in new business projects. Some **investors** grew wealthy. So did the banks, who charged interest. The amount of businesses increased. However, the Catholic Church and Islam thought that lending money for interest was a sin, called **usury**.

" Usury [lending money] makes a gain out of money itself, and not from the natural use or purpose of money. "

Greek philosopher Aristotle, 400s B.C.E.

Food and Dress

As trade increased wealth, more people had the time and money to take more interest in the food they ate and the clothes they wore.

THE LURE OF SPICES

☞ **Makes bad food taste good!**

☞ **Opens trade routes**

Spices are seeds, fruits, roots, or bark that add flavor and color to other foods. Spices are also used to make medicine, cosmetics, and perfume. They became popular in Europe during the Middle Ages. In particular, they helped disguise the taste of old food. Most spices were rare, so they were expensive. The most expensive was saffron (right). It took 70,000 saffron flowers to make a pound of spice. As most spices came from Asia, European merchants looked for new trade routes there.

THE HEIGHT OF FASHION

✦ **Who's that in the hat?**

In the later Middle Ages, rich people began to show off their wealth in their fashions. They regularly changed the style of their clothes simply because they could afford to do so. Sometimes new styles were taken to extremes. This happened with the hennin (above, left). Noblewomen began to wear this cone-shaped headdress around 1430. It became the fashion to exaggerate its height, with some headdresses eventually reaching 2.6 feet (80 cm)!

ENGLAND'S SHEEP

+ Wool makes money

England had ideal grassland for breeding sheep. Wool from the sheep was in demand from textile makers in Netherlands, France, and Italy. English landowners began fencing off land normally farmed by peasants so they could raise more sheep. This process increased unemployment, and left less room to grow food crops such as grain.

A NEW SOURCE OF FISH

- Fishing on the Grand Banks
- Europeans cross the Atlantic

Fish was a popular food in the Middle Ages. The Vikings were catching cod by 800. They learned how to preserve the fish by drying it. Catholics ate fish on Fridays, when they were forbidden from eating meat. This created a demand for dried cod throughout Europe. Fishing fleets in search of cod sailed far into the Atlantic Ocean. In the 1500s, the Basques of northern Spain discovered the Grand Banks off Newfoundland (left). There were so many cod in the ocean, fishers said they could catch them just by lowering a bucket into the water.

THE FASHION OF FUR

+ Nobles demand the best

Early in the Middle Ages, fur was seen as a "barbarian" form of dress. That changed in the 900s. Wealthy Europeans began to wear furs such as **ermine**, sable, marten, lynx, and beaver. The softer the fur, the more it cost. Peasants wore cheaper rabbit, goat, and wolf skins. The demand for fur was so high that some species were hunted to extinction. Merchants looked for new sources of fur in Russia.

The Lap of Luxury

Trade and the money it earned began to change the way people lived their lives. Large numbers of people could enjoy fine goods from around the world.

SMOOTH AS SILK

+ Treasure from the East...

+ ...but only for nobles

One of the most popular imports to Europe was silk. The fabric was made from the cocoons of silkworms that could only be found in the Middle East and East Asia. Silk was smooth and light, yet strong. It was woven in bold colors with vibrant patterns. Wealthy Europeans were eager to dress in the new cloth. Silk clothing became a status symbol for kings and lords—and the merchants who supplied it became rich.

BREAKING NEWS

Have you heard about the fashionable new windows? European inventors have found a way to make colored glass quickly and cheaply. This **stained glass** is being used in the windows of churches. It is cut into pieces and put together to illustrate Bible stories (right). In Germany, plain glass is produced in sheets. Try using large panes of this glass in your windows. You won't believe how full of light your home will be!

ALL THAT GLITTERS!

- ☛ Gold and silver in demand
- ☛ Metals easier to obtain

In the early Middle Ages, miners looked for iron, which could be made into tools and armor. After the 900s, **metallurgists** learned to produce metals more efficiently. It became cheaper and easier to mine copper, gold, and silver from the ground. As merchants grew wealthier, they wanted to buy precious metals in the form of artworks or jewelry.

Did you know?

In the 1500s, a German scholar named Georg Agricola wrote a book about metals and how they were extracted from rocks. He is known as the "Father of Metallurgy."

WELCOME TO MY HOME

- ☛ No more castles

The later Middle Ages were a relatively peaceful time. In the early Middle Ages, kings and nobles had built castles for protection. Now, merchants and traders built homes that were comfortable and that showed off their wealth. Kings and nobles struggled to pay to upgrade their castles to keep up with the fashions of the new country houses (left).

CHANGE HOW YOU DRESS!

- ✦ Laws control clothing
- ✦ Displaying rank through dress

Some kings tried to stop rich merchants from dressing like nobles. They introduced **sumptuary laws**. King Edward III of England made laws that told people what to wear according to their rank. Non-Christians, such as Muslims and Jews, also had to wear special clothes. From 1215, Jewish men had to wear a special cone-shaped hat (left).

The Silk Road

Medieval trade routes stretched from Europe to Asia and parts of Africa. Chinese jade, Indian spices, Persian textiles, and German furs were traded over long distances.

TRADING CITIES

+ **Great cities control trade**

+ **Merchants meet there**

Few merchants traveled the whole length of a trade route. On the long routes across Asia, European traders used **middlemen**. The middlemen traveled parts of a route for merchants, selling goods to other merchants. This made it easier for European or Chinese merchants to obtain foreign goods. Merchants met at cities such as Samarkand (right), in modern-day Uzbekistan. These trading cities remained rich until trade between Europe and China shifted to sea rather than land routes.

AN ANCIENT NETWORK

✦ **Trade routes established for centuries**

✦ **Named for silk**

Trade links between Europe and China existed before the Middle Ages. China traded with Central Asia from around 2000 B.C.E. By 200 B.C.E. the routes reached as far as modern-day Turkey and Europe. The routes were known together as the Silk Road, because Chinese silk was one of the main goods that passed to Europe along that route. Other frequently traded goods included **porcelain** and horses.

NEWS FROM AFAR

One stop on the Silk Road was Baghdad in modern-day Iraq. Baghdad became a hub of learning. The House of Wisdom (right) was established there by the Islamic ruler Harun al-Rashid. The House of Wisdom was a center for academics who studied ancient Greek, Persian, and Syrian books. The books helped preserve the works of ancient philosophers.

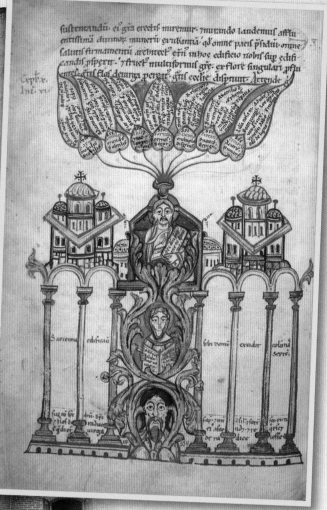

A USEFUL PEACE

☛ Mongols impose order

The Mongol Empire set up in the 1200s stretched from China to eastern Europe. It included most of the Silk Road. Mongol forces protected travelers from thieves. More travelers started using the Silk Road. Special safe stopping places or roadside inns named *caravanserais* (above) were built for merchants and their animals to rest along the route.

KEY ROUTE

+ Silk Road not just for goods

+ Spreads ideas and disease

The Silk Road did not only carry goods. It also carried ideas and religions. In East Asia, **Buddhism** had spread from India to China along the Silk Road in the ancient world. In the Middle Ages, Muslim traders from the Middle East carried the Islamic faith east into Asia. They spread Islam among the local traders they met. Islam was widely adopted in Central Asia and in places such as Indonesia. The Silk Road also carried disease. In the 1340s, it provided the route for the Black Death to travel from Central Asia to Europe.

The Trade Routes

Trading was not always easy. Merchants faced tolls, dishonest traders, and years away from home, as well as the risk of thieves, pirates, and shipwrecks.

Discoveries

In Europe's "Age of Discovery," explorers headed west to seek a new route to China and Asia. Instead, they explored North and South America.

BARRIERS TO TRADE

+ **Competition leads to taxes**

+ **And also to wars**

Some kingdoms tried to protect their own industries against cheaper goods made elsewhere. They imposed a tariff or tax to make **imports** more expensive, or banned the trade altogether. In Italy, Venice and Genoa fought to control trade. Each captured the others' trading ships at sea, and they fought over ports such as Chioggia (right).

TRADE AND WARFARE

✦ **Increased business**

War was good and bad for trade. War increased the demand for weapons and armor. The **Crusades** made the Europeans build bigger ships to transport soldiers to the Holy Land (left). That led to bigger and faster trading ships. However, traders risked being attacked by pirates fighting on behalf of different warring kingdoms.

TRADE WITH THE ISLAMIC EMPIRE

✦ Europeans and Muslims trade

The Islamic Empire controlled the overland routes to India and China. Ports on the eastern Mediterranean such as Constantinople (below) were centers for silks, spices, and textiles. Arabian traders traded with Europeans, Indians, Persians, and Africans. Even when Muslims and Europeans fought over the Holy Land in the Crusades, trade between the two sides continued.

My Medieval Journal

Imagine you are a merchant in Venice during the Crusades. Many Christians are at war in the Holy Land, but you want to keep trading with your Muslim contacts. Write a letter to the rulers of Venice explaining the reasons for your decision.

Did you know?

Constantinople was conquered by the Muslim Ottoman Turks in 1453. They renamed the city Istanbul. The event is often seen as marking the end of the Middle Ages.

VOYAGES OF DISCOVERY

☞ Europeans sail the world

In the early 1400s, the Portuguese traveled south down the coast of Africa. They were trying to bypass the Islamic Empire and find a sea route to the Indian Ocean. Sailors from other countries sailed west, hoping to reach China from the east. They did not know that America lay in their way. Europe's take-over of North America (right) was a key step in European **colonization** of the world.

Changing the World

History often features dramatic events such as wars or revolutions. However, trade and the links it creates between people have played a huge role in shaping history.

BREAKING NEWS

Have you noticed that trade does not only spread goods? It also spreads knowledge! The writings of ancient Greeks such as Aristotle have reached Europe from the Islamic Empire. Europeans now do math with Arabic numbers (which actually came from India). Buddhism has also spread along the Silk Road from its birthplace in India. There are now Buddhist monasteries in China (above). Wherever people meet, they exchange ideas as well as goods— and we are all richer because of it.

ISLAM IN ASIA

+ Sufis convert local peoples...

+ ...gain many followers

Trade helped the Islamic faith to spread from the Middle East. Arabian traders took the religion to India and southeast Asia, sharing their ideas along with the goods they sold. **Missionaries** called Sufis followed the traders to Asia. They persuaded the ruling classes of Asian kingdoms to become Muslims. By 1136, Islam had spread as far as Indonesia.

TRADING IN SLAVES

◆ **Millions sold into slavery**

In the Middle Ages, people were widely traded as slaves by Asians, Muslims, and Europeans. There was little control over the trade. In Egypt, Christian slaves were forced to convert to Islam. They were trained as soldiers (right) and sent to fight Christian powers. These so-called Mamluks later came to rule Egypt themselves.

RISE AND FALL

☞ **Cities and kingdoms flourish...**

☞ **...and then decline**

Trade routes made many cities such as Venice (left) and Genoa rich and powerful. As trade routes changed, however, cities that had once been wealthy fell into decline. When the Ottoman Empire closed the Silk Road after 1453, the previously wealthy trading center of Samarkand lost its power and the city faded into history.

A NEW ECONOMIC FORCE

+ **Changing how Europe thinks**

Merchants and trade changed much in the Middle Ages. Bankers such as the Bardi family loaned money to kings to pay for wars. They loaned money to merchants to pay for journeys to new lands. These traders came across ideas that changed how Europeans thought. The way people had lived in the early Middle Ages no longer made sense. A period of great change had begun in Europe—and it would affect the whole world.

Glossary

apprentices Junior workers learning a trade from a skilled employer

bankrupt Unable to pay one's debts

Buddhism A religion founded in India by the Buddha in the 6th century B.C.E.

charters Written documents that give bodies such as towns certain rights

colonies Countries or areas controlled by another country

colonization The process of starting colonies

Crusades A series of religious wars fought between Christians and Muslims for control of the Holy Land

epidemics Widespread outbreaks of disease

ermine The white winter fur of a stoat

feudal society A social organization in which all land is held in return for service to a king or a lord

forge A blacksmith's workshop

fraudulent Based on deception

guilds Associations of merchants or craftsmen

hostlers People employed to look after travelers' horses

imports Goods from another country

interest A fee charged by a lender for making a loan

investors People who pay for a scheme in the hope of making a profit if it succeeds

merchants People who trade in goods

metallurgists People who work with metals

middlemen People who buy goods from a supplier and sell them to merchants

mint A place where money is made

missionaries People who spread a religion in a foreign land

nobles People who hold a high rank in a feudal society and pass it on to their family

persecute To treat a group of people badly because of their religion, color, or gender

plague A severe, usually fatal disease

porcelain A fine type of china

sheriff An official in charge of town government

stereotype A widely held but simplified and untrue idea about a type of person

sumptuary laws Laws that try to restrict what people can buy, wear, or consume

textile A type of cloth or woven fabric

tradespeople People who work in skilled trades, such as making things or buying and selling goods

usury In Catholic teaching, the sin of charging interest on a loan

---

European nobles begin to wear fur. Some animals are hunted to extinction.

A rise in trade and a growth of towns begins throughout Europe.

The Pope orders Jews and Muslims to wear special clothes to identify themselves.

Marco Polo leaves Venice for China.

900s — **1000** — **1100** — **1215** — **1256** — **1271**

About now, European craftspeople learn how to make stained glass.

About now, regular trade fairs in Champagne become important economic events.

Venice and Genoa fight the first of six wars over trade.

On the Web

medievaleurope.mrdonn.org/index.html
This site has information about medieval trades, fashions, and famous people of the time, with quizzes and games.

www.historyforkids.net/medieval-daily-life.html
A page about daily life in the Middle Ages, with links to many more pages about the medieval period.

www.medieval-life-and-times.info/medieval-life/medieval-fairs.htm
A page about trade fairs and the role they played in medieval life.

www.ducksters.com/history/middle_ages_guilds.php
A page about guilds and why they became so important for medieval craftsmen and merchants.

Books

Elliott, Lynne. *Medieval Towns, Trade, and Travel*. Crabtree Publishing, 2004.

Hull, Robert. *Merchant* (Medieval Lives). Franklin Watts, 2008.

Macdonald, Fiona. *Travel and Trade in the Middle Ages* (World Almanac Library of the Middle Ages). Gareth Stevens, 2006.

Twist, Clint. *Marco Polo: History's Great Adventurer* (Historical Notebooks). Candlewick, 2011.

Watson, Danielle. *The City in Medieval Europe* (Life in Medieval Europe). Cavendish Square Publishing, 2016.

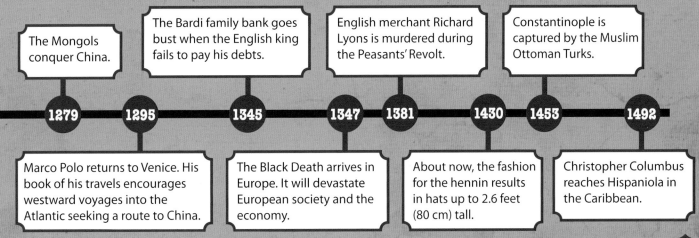

The Mongols conquer China.

The Bardi family bank goes bust when the English king fails to pay his debts.

English merchant Richard Lyons is murdered during the Peasants' Revolt.

Constantinople is captured by the Muslim Ottoman Turks.

1279 1295 1345 1347 1381 1430 1453 1492

Marco Polo returns to Venice. His book of his travels encourages westward voyages into the Atlantic seeking a route to China.

The Black Death arrives in Europe. It will devastate European society and the economy.

About now, the fashion for the hennin results in hats up to 2.6 feet (80 cm) tall.

Christopher Columbus reaches Hispaniola in the Caribbean.

Index